The 10 Most Common Estate Planning Mistakes and How to Avoid Them

Post Taxpayer's Relief Act of 2013

Testimonials

Because of all the previous uncertainty in estate planning law, I was frozen. I knew I needed to do some proactive planning, but I just couldn't get moving. Then I read David's The Ten Most Common Estate Planning Mistakes, had his firm analyze my estate and provide me my personal road map. I am glad to report, I finally have a solid complete estate plan in place for my posterity.
Judy and Charles T., California

I was always so confused about what my next steps would be to proper estate planning. David's book has really cleared things up.
Roger L., New York

"We found the Estate Analysis to be very helpful. When a person adds up all his personal items (real estate, cars, etc.), he finds his estate to be much larger than expected.

David T. Phillips

The IRS never said thank you for all the taxes I've paid them, so I'd hate to see my children pay them any more when we die." Marlin F., Mexico, MO

I don't have much of an estate, but what I do have I wanted my grandchildren to get it. For a multitude of lame excuses I just didn't take the time to formulate a logical distribution strategy. Then I read Mr. Phillips' book The 10 Most Common Estate Planning Mistakes. I was making 7 of the mistakes. That alone motivated me into action. Steve and Rene W., AZ

Acknowledgements

Because of the constant changes in tax law, this book has experienced several editions through the years. On **January 2, 2013**, Congress was forced to pass The American Taxpayer's Relief Act. President Obama signed it into law the very next day. The changes in the estate planning world were so sweeping that I was compelled to publish this 2013 revision.

Many have helped to bring this book to a reality and I wish to thank them: My son, D. Todd Phillips, the president of our firm, Estate Planning Specialists for his technological assistance, his knowledge, his input and his faith. Richard Durfee, founder and senior partner of The Durfee Law Group, for his legal advice, his keen eye and his help with our many clients. Isaac Valenzuela, founder of NV Design, for his graphic design of the covers. Lora Hansen, for preparing the hundreds of Estate Analysis through the

David T. Phillips

years, giving us real life stories to tell. My wife Jane, for taking the time to read and re-read the manuscript. And most important, to Sara Grace Waddell, for putting together all of the pieces. You truly are a master.

I also want to express special gratitude to financial experts: Dr. Mark Skousen (*Forecast & Strategies*), Dr. David Eifrig (*Retirement Millionaire*), Bob Carlson (*Retirement Watch*), Tony Sagami (*Asian Alert*), and Financial Columnist Terry Savage for repeatedly recommending me and my firm to their readers. Thanks to all.

To my beautiful grandchildren

My goal is to leave you a grand financial legacy, an interesting personal legacy and most important a powerful spiritual legacy, because I love you all so much.

David T. Phillips

Contents

David T. Phillips

Special Note to Reader

Congratulations. By obtaining this book you have taken the first and most important step towards planning your estate – gaining knowledge. Nothing is more critical in the struggle to *keep your wealth in the family.*

By reading *The Ten Most Common Estate Planing Mistakes* and its companion book *Estate Planning Made Easy* (www.epmez.com) you will learn how to properly safeguard your assets from creditors, predators and the IRS.

Upon death, legal fees, income taxes, federal estate taxes, state inheritance taxes and other estate settlement costs often strip more than 70% of the assets intended for your family. To ensure that your family receives what you've worked so hard to accumulate in the way you want, you need to

David T. Phillips

implement a concrete plan that will make certain your legacy will be a perpetual legacy.

In this book, I've identified the TEN mistakes that, in my opinion, are the most grievous and the most common. Fortunately, they are easy to avoid. What follows is an overview of these errors along with viable solutions that can be implemented so that when you pass on, your estate ends up where it belongs – in the hands of your loved ones.

Good Reading,

David T. Phillips, CEO
Estate Planning Specialists

Introduction

Do you remember the short story of Rip Van Winkle as told by George Washington Irving? Van Winkle goes to sleep after a game of bowling and much drinking in the mountains with a band of dwarves. He awakens twenty years later, an old man. Back home, Rip finds that all has changed: his wife is dead, his daughter is married, and the American Revolutionary War has taken place.

Since the passage of the Economic Growth Tax Relief Reconciliation Act in mid 2001 (EGTRRA), the majority of wealthy Americans have been using Rip Van Winkle as their role model. It seems that because estate taxation rules have been in flux, they have been content to sleep it off and wait until they wake up to do any estate planning. BIG MISTAKE!

David T. Phillips

First and foremost, estate planning is so much more than just taxes. It is the premeditated decision to determine who gets what, when they get it, and how they get it. It is a true act of love and respect for those we leave behind. But if it is so important, why do 72% of today's affluent avoid estate planning altogether?

There is a litany of reasons, but top on the list is procrastination. Estate planning isn't an exciting task – that's true – but it's vital to the sanctity of the family. Archeologists have proven the ancient Egyptians wrong – YOU CAN'T TAKE IT WITH YOU! We all need an estate plan.

Another reason why only a small percentage plan their estate is that it appears confusing. Considering that the estate and pension tax laws have changed three times in the last five years, it's no wonder we're afraid and would rather put it off. My overall goal in writing this book, publishing my book *Estate Planning Made Easy* and the existence of my firm, Estate Planning Specialists, LLC, with select advisors throughout the country, is to make the complex easy to understand and implement.

I realize that politicians would have us believe that estate planning is all about estate taxes, but it isn't.

Avoiding probate fees, the proper use of your estate tax exclusions, properly stretching IRA/pension accounts, guaranteeing dollars tomorrow by leveraging pennies today, financially preparing for a long term medical illness, guaranteeing income for life, getting the equity out of your home while staying there, The Wealth Creation Strategy, the IRA Leverage Strategy, The Wealth Replacement Strategy, The Family Bank Strategy, medical power of attorney, personal guardianship, philanthropy – these are just a few of the reasons why proper estate planning is crucial and shouldn't be something to sleep on.

In Rip Van Winkle, George Washington Irving told the story of an old man ill prepared for his departure, and a man who gets a second chance to make things right even after a long sleep. Now with the passage of The Tax Payer's Relief Act of 2012, it is time to wake up, switch off the "snooze button" and take affirmative action. Your legacy depends on it. **Remember: Procrastination is dangerous to your wealth!**

David T. Phillips

Mistake 1:

Failure to have any plan at all, or having an antiquated or improper plan.

We often hear of families torn apart because a parent or grandparent fails to predetermine who gets what. "She wanted me to have it," claims one child. "No she didn't, she promised it to me," retorts another. Who is right? Only the deceased knows for certain. Too bad she didn't write it down. Too bad she didn't take a few minutes to let her true wishes known.

At a time when we want the best feelings to exist, when we want them to find comfort in each others' arms, family members, out of selfishness, can foster the worst

"At a minimum, all estate planning documents should be reviewed every five years."

traits in the spectrum of human emotions. Anger, envy, jealousy – even hate – can be found when confusion is wrought because of a failure to preplan the distribution of even the most modest estate. Sins of omission are still sins.

Antiquated plans are just as problematic. A will drawn up 10 years ago is unlikely to reflect your current situation. Think of how much happens during that time. In fact, I have seen more problems resulting from outdated wills than any other situation. New marriages, new domiciles, new tax laws, growth, more children and grandchildren, retirement income, new investments; the reasons to update your plan are endless. Anyone who has a will or a revocable living trust that hasn't been reviewed since the passage of the Tax Relief Act of 2010 is asking for serious trouble. At a minimum, all estate planning documents should be reviewed every five years.

Improper plans also create problems, such as do-it-yourself kits that are never completely finished, non-funded revocable living trusts and/or multiple conflicting wills. All you accomplish with an improper plan is to create confusion, making life

David T. Phillips

difficult down the road for your heirs, encouraging disputes.

Solution:

The way to rectify these problems is to follow Nike's advice: **"Just do it!"** But do what? Where do you start? The first step with any foreign subject and new adventure is to gain an education. You shouldn't walk into an estate planning attorney's office and say," OK, I'm ready, plan my estate for me." Not only would that be a pricey mistake, you will end up with a plan that's not really yours.

Where do you get an education? You've already taken a major step in the right direction by reading this book. Other books, such as my *Estate Planning Made Easy* (recently updated and in its Fourth Edition), are written to help the layperson make sense out of estate planning strategies. You can also visit our website, **www.epmez.com**.

Seminars are also a great source of ideas. But take heed: attend with an open mind, not an open checkbook. Many presenters push their CD's and books with very little else to offer. Be careful. If you buy a lecture series, make certain you plan on listening to them. If not, you could waste hundreds of dollars that could have been better used to properly plan your estate.

Another word of caution: many seminars are given by estate planning hacks whose sole objective is to sell you an annuity or a "one-size-fits-all" Revocable Living Trust. Make certain that the "expert" is indeed an "expert" and that an estate planning attorney with credentials is part of the planning process.

Just Do It! Properly plan your estate. If you don't, the IRS and probate courts will do it for you. I guarantee you, it won't be in your best interest or your family's. You have the power now to decide what kind of legacy you want to leave your heirs. Take control by being proactive and implementing your wishes – not the government's.

David T. Phillips

Mistake 2:

Believing that The American Taxpayer Relief Act of 2012 will actually provide tax relief

I don't know about you but after celebrating a wonderful Christmas this past year with my family, of major concern was how Congress was going to avert the so-called Fiscal Cliff. In an unprecedented fashion the Senate reconvened on New Year's Day, and in the early morning hours passed The American Taxpayer Relief Act of 2012 (ATRA). Then hours later the House approved the bill after the spending cut provisions were abandoned.

The joke of the day says it all: How do you know if a politician is lying? Answer: "His lips are moving." Congress and the President know all too well that ATRA provided very little relief. In fact the name is one of grandest oxy morons of our day. The only apparent relief came in the estate tax arena.

Because the federal estate and gift tax exclusions were set to be reduced to $1,000,000 at midnight on December 31, 2012, Congress was forced to make a move. As part of ATRA both exclusions were set at $5,000,000, indexed for inflation ($5,250,000 in 2013), with a top 40% federal estate tax rate for assets greater than the exclusion. At first blush it looks like relief, but Congress and the President aren't finished.

One constant that I know as an estate planner for the past 40 years is that tax laws are never permanent. I have seen the estate tax exclusion as low as $60,000 and the top estate tax bracket as high as 75%. Because of the gigantic deficit, the growing government monster needs revenue. They have pledged to tax the main source of wealth in the country.....the rich and small businesses, so don't expect outrage or sympathy from the press as taxes increase.

Don't be lulled into a false sense of security. Plan your estates immediately. Don't wait another minute. The other shoe has not yet fallen. The estate and gift

David T. Phillips

tax exclusion increase was a bone that was thrown to the media. It looks good and benevolent and yet it only affected a few families either way. Don't rest easy.

A few days after ATRA was signed into law Nancy Pelosi proclaimed, "we are not done raising taxes." President Obama said as much the following Saturday during his radio address while vacationing in Hawaii. How will they raise taxes? By sleight of hand. Magic.

With the elimination of certain deductions, exemptions, credits, etc., taxes can be increased. One minute you have it and the next you don't. Last year President Obama released his Green Book proposals with a litany of desired changes to many popular planning tools used by affluent Americans, most of which would raise revenues without raising tax rates. The Obama Green Book proposals include:

- Elimination of the non-spousal "lifetime stretch option" currently available for all inherited qualified accounts (IRA, 401k, etc.), with a complete distribution over a maximum of 5 years;

- Minimum term of 10 years for Grantor Retained Annuity Trusts;
- Limitation on the number of years you may skip generations;
- Elimination of the valuation discounts associated with intra-family asset sales and gifts;
- The inclusion of the entire value of a Grantor Trust in one's taxable estate.
- The loss of the tax-free step-up in basis on appreciated assets at death. Currently we can transfer all capital gains to our family at death, tax free. While the estate tax exclusion may be beyond the reach of most estates, the elimination of the step-up in basis would seriously impact most estates.

With the passage of The American Taxpayer Relief Act one may logically put their guard down. Don't be duped into believing that you now have plenty of time to plan because the estate and gift tax exclusions are supposedly permanent at a lofty $5 million. If you haven't already done so, have all of your planning options put in place now. DO NOT WAIT!

The Obama administration has shown their hand. They are not going to stop trying to raise revenue (code word for "taxes") to offset spending cuts. Forewarned should be forearmed.

One last word of warning: When planning your estate don't forget state inheritance taxes. Currently 26 states impose a tax on transferred assets at death, some as high as 19%. The state of your domicile at the time of your death determines whether of now you will be taxed! Failure to plan for this tax could have serious financial consequences.

Solution:

First, have your estate professionally analyzed. An unbiased personalized Estate Analysis can give you a peek into the future by taking a snapshot of your assets today, calculate your net worth, and then offer personalized suggestions on which strategies would work best for you in order to maximize your estate and minimize estate shrinkage due to federal and state estate and income taxes. A well-thought-out Estate Analysis can be the road map that guides you toward proper estate planning, allowing you to keep your wealth in the family, while maintaining control.

Competent estate planners are generally well equipped to do such an analysis. **Estate Planning Specialists, LLC** has analyzed over 5,000 estates of every size from every state of the union. To complete your analysis profile form and order your own comprehensive personalized Estate Analysis simply go to our website: www.epmez.com, or call toll free 1-888-892-1102.

David T. Phillips

Mistake 3:

Blindly leaving everything to your spouse because of "portability"

Since the Tax Act of 1981 and the introduction of the 100% marital deduction, 80% of America's affluent have elected to pass their total estate to their surviving spouse, usually the wife. In fact, for a joint estate valued in excess of $5.25 million in 2013 or an estate with the potential to appreciate beyond that figure, not passing everything to your spouse will be the most expensive and needless mistake you will ever make. To put it in dollars and cents, currently an individual estate valued at $6 million will pay over $300,000 in needless federal estate taxes. The estate of a married couple valued at $10.5 million will generate an estate tax of zero. If you are married, you should maximize the generosity of the government by using both the exclusions. In that case, any federal estate taxes you pay are voluntary and unnecessary.

A provision known as "portability" was introduced with The Tax Act of 2010 and reconfirmed with the passage of the recent American Taxpayer Relief Act of 2012. Simply stated "portability" allows a couple to use both federal estate tax exclusions regardless of when the survivor passes away. Many could fall prey to this deceptive strategy and not plan their estates, believing that even if their estates grow to $10 million no federal estate taxes would be due. On the surface "portability" may appear tantalizing, but there are so many reasons why we shouldn't use it to substitute proper planning.

Solution:

Based on current law, everyone has the right to pass up to $5.25 million in property value, free from federal estate taxes. It is vital that each spouse use this exclusion. That's $10.5 million per couple, and it is money that can also pass from one generation to the next totally free of federal estate taxes. The most effective way to make certain that you maximize this

David T. Phillips

tax-saving strategy is to establish, prior to the death of the first spouse, a Revocable Family Dynasty Trust with credit shelter trust (CST) provisions.

Upon death of the first spouse, assets valued in excess of the current estate tax exclusion are placed into the Credit Shelter Trust (CST), also known as a By-Pass, or B Trust. The surviving spouse is not the trustee. The survivor can, however, access 5% of the trust's funds, all the interest, and whatever is needed for health, education and general support. Of course, they can live on their share of the estate however they please. For a graphic example of how the Revocable Family Dynasty Trust with CST provisions works, see Figure 1.

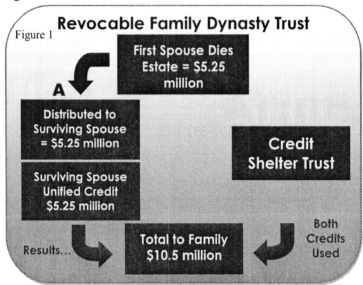

Figure 1

Revocable Family Dynasty Trust

First Spouse Dies
Estate = $5.25 million

A

Distributed to Surviving Spouse = $5.25 million

Surviving Spouse Unified Credit $5.25 million

Credit Shelter Trust

Results...

Total to Family $10.5 million

Both Credits Used

While a CST can be established through testamentary provisions in a will, most competent estate planners concur that the Revocable Family Dynasty Trust (RFDT) with a CST works best, leaving nothing to chance, or the political winds.

A few uninformed planners suggest that because of the "portability" provision and given the fact that the federal estate tax exclusion is $5.25 million a Credit Shelter Trust isn't needed. I asked Richard Durfee, founder of The Durfee Law Group, a national estate and asset protection law firm, to list the reasons why following the "portability" trap is such a bad idea. Here are his answers:

- Portability merely makes the exclusion portable between spouses, nothing else. – the biggest effect is that a couple can have a single joint trust and hold their assets in common – provided it has credit shelter provisions, even in separate property states;
- All assets transferred to the B trust at the passing of the first spouse will not be subject to future estate taxes. If $2 million is transferred it

is always valued at $2 million for estate taxes even if it grows to $20 million;

- You still have to make an election even with portability;
- You still have to file The IRS Estate Tax Form 706 with portability;
- You still have to have a means of administering the exclusion even with portability;
- RFDT provides the means of administration;
- A Credit Shelter Trust can permit the surviving spouse to retain an income interest and control over the assets, whereas they would otherwise just pass to the deceased spouse's heirs;
- A Credit Shelter trust can allocate and administer the deceased spouse's Generation Skip Transfer exclusion;
- A Credit Shelter trust may provide for some asset protection for the surviving spouse if properly crafted;
- A Credit Shelter trust may provide for Medicaid planning for the surviving spouse;
- A Credit Shelter trust can be part of "dynasty" planning which plans for protecting wealth over

multiple generations, not just dealing with death and related taxes.

Ten convincing reasons why you should ignore the politicians' attempt to deceive Americans into believing that we don't need to plan our estates. As is evident, even modest estates should include an A/B Credit Shelter Trust as part of their FDT or Revocable Living Trust. Furthermore, and most important as I stated earlier, estate planning is much more than estate taxes. It is planning the logical distribution of your assets, no matter how much or how little that may be.

Another concern I often hear is that sudden wealth through inheritance can spoil children and grandchildren. While we've all heard such horror stories, mostly in novels like John Grisham's book, *The Testament* or celebrity dramatics, they can be eliminated altogether with proper planning. Most problems are a result of zero planning. Competent estate planning attorneys recommend the establishment of incentive clauses in a trust. For example, it can be stipulated that a beneficiary's inheritance be received after certain life goals are achieved; such as, an annual income level, a college degree, marriage, etc. Age

David T. Phillips

factors should also be considered, but not be the only provision. Of course, such clauses may not be needed if your heirs are older or are capable of handling an inheritance.

I recommend a simple Revocable Living Trust (RLT) for estates under $500,000 and a Revocable Family Dynasty Trust (RFDT) for larger estates. Many fret over the up-front costs of such vehicles, and so they put it off and allow probate expenses to be assessed at death, usually 5% to 10% of the gross estate value. Financial tightness today will cost thousands tomorrow.

For example, a proper attorney crafted RLT costs around $3,000 and a RFDT, $4,000. An estate comprising of a home valued at $300,000 with a $150,000 mortgage, a $200,000 investment account and real estate of $200,000, would have an estimated probate expense of $35,000. ($300,000 + $200,000 + $200,000 = $700,000 total gross estate x .05% in probate fees = $35,000). A properly designed RFDT is only $4,000, a savings to your family of $31,000!

For readers of this book we have negotiated special discounted fees for Revocable Living Trusts and Revocable Family Dynasty Trusts with The Durfee Law Group. Simply contact them at 480-324-8000 or rick@durfeelawgroup.com to obtain their easy-to-complete profile and fact finder. Mention this book: *The Ten Most Common Estate Planning Mistakes* to receive your discount.

David T. Phillips

Mistake 4:

Paying too much income and capital gains tax

In an ideal world we would all pay the same percentage for the services we receive from our governments. But unfortunately the biggest burden seems to always land on the shoulders of the affluent. With the incomprehensible national debt, the re-election of President Obama and the increase in "big government," it is no secret that taxes on our earned and unearned income (investments) are about to increase.

The recent American Taxpayer Relief Act, actually increased taxes in many key areas:

- Estate and gift taxes increased from the 35% top rate in 2012 to 40% for the foreseeable future;
- Income taxes to a new top rate of 39.6% for income over $400,000 for single filers, $425,000 for head-of-household filers and $450,000 for married taxpayers filing jointly.
- Capital gains and dividends increased from 15% to 20% for top income earners
- All taxpayers will see a 2% income tax increase (return to 6.2% from 4.2%) in the employee portion of the Social Security tax.
- The Health Care Surtax of 3.8% will be imposed on earned and investment income for taxpayers with income of $250,000 (joint) and $200,000 (single).

The Fiscal Cliff's, American Taxpayer Relief Act was just a first blush attempt at raising revenue. The message from Washington is clear, "we are not done increasing taxes!"

The more we pay in taxes the less we will have in our estates. A grave mistake that most of us fall prey to is that we simply pay too much. It is always wise to pay as little as legally possible, but the loop holes are closing and for those on salary, the wiggle room is tiny. For most the only tax saving area we have is with our investments. We need to find investments that do not incur a tax on the gains and the eventual income.

Solution:

The first option to consider is tax deferred investments, those include: qualified accounts like an IRA or 401k and Single Premium Deferred Annuities. The problem with these deferred investments is that eventually income taxes have to be paid on the gain or the profit. Furthermore, if you die holding these deferred assets, your beneficiaries will be required to pay the income tax, sur taxes and of course the estate tax, both federal and state.

What compounds this problem is that your beneficiaries do not receive a "step-up-in-basis" and their inherited deferred taxed asset will incur an income tax in the year following your death that will be added to their current tax liability. Just imagine for a moment; your $500,000 IRA drops into the lap of your attorney son who is already making a good living. This income infusion can throw your beneficiaries into the highest bracket overnight.

The second option is to defer more income today for distribution at a later date when your income is less. Again qualified accounts like an IRA or traditional deferred compensation plans like a 401k allow you to take income off the top and have it accumulate in a tax deferred environment. It is important that you take full advantage of these strategies because they could lower your top line income to a lower bracket. The problem is that the maximum limits are relatively small and can have little impact on the high wage earner.

If you are self-employed and have few employees you should consider a 412e3 deferred account because it allows you to take a significantly greater amount of income off the top line ($200,000-$300,000) than the traditional IRA, SEP IRA or defined benefit plans. The more you take off the top, the lower your bracket, resulting in a lower tax today. Interest will accumulate tax deferred, but as with all deferred accounts, taxes will have to be paid when you access the funds or when they are passed to your beneficiaries.

David T. Phillips

Another suggestion for the self-employed is to begin your own welfare benefit plan, also known as a Section 419 qualified account. With the 419 plan you take current income off the top line and transfer it into an account that allows you to prepay your post retirement medical expenses. The funds accumulate tax-free and can be extracted at retirement, tax-free as long as they are used to fund a generous list of medical expenses (health spas, health insurance premiums, medication, long term medical expenses, etc).

The third option is to invest in real estate and stock investments. As your investments appreciate in value no taxes are due. Of course you pay current income taxes on the rental income and dividends, but no taxes are due until you sell the asset. At that time either short or long term capital gains taxes will be assessed depending on how long you held the asset. You could continually defer capital gains on this type of investment by never selling it and based on current law, when you pass it to your heirs they would receive a step-up-in-basis, only paying capital gains tax on going-forward appreciation from the day it was inherited.

The fourth option is to find investments that spin off income and provide healthy income tax offsets, like oil and gas partnerships. Beneficiaries currently will receive a step-up-in-basis so that any capital gains will be calculated based on the current value of the asset when it is inherited.

The fifth option is to invest in precious metals and collectibles. Currently, if the price of precious metals or collectibles increase, no taxes are incurred until they are sold. There is a higher capital gains tax due for collectibles, so usually these types of investments are better for the long haul. If metals or collectibles are passed to a beneficiary they currently receive a step-up-in-basis.

The sixth option and frankly one of the most sensible and one that is available to all wage earners, is to invest in life insurance. I know this may be a hard pill to swallow for some, but in reality it is the **only** investment in the country that allows for *tax-free growth*, *tax-free income* and a supercharged life insurance benefit that can be passed to your beneficiaries totally *income tax* and *estate tax free*.

In the past, life insurance has been relatively boring, but effective none-the-less. Today, with the advent of Indexed Universal Life improved participating Whole Life policies and the *Family Bank Strategy* life insurance has come into its' own and in my opinion is the best "safe-money" financial vehicle available, packed with superior tax advantages. I cover this option in detail in **Mistake 8**, *Lacking Liquidity to Cover Estate Settlement Expenses.*

Mistake 5:

Not properly using the IRS-approved annual and lifetime gift allowances

The vast majority of affluent Americans don't comprehend the need to share their wealth with their loved ones while they are still alive. Furthermore, they don't understand the power that "leverage" can create and the many tax benefits that can and will be realized if they apply this simple concept. In fact, in most cases, by leveraging the IRS gift allowance, all estate shrinkage can be totally eliminated. Yet only a handful of prudent taxpayers utilize this basic, but powerful, strategy.

Each and every American can, by current law, gift $14,000 annually – completely tax free – to anyone they want. I often joke in estate planning seminars that

David T. Phillips

I can legally drive up to a homeless man on the corner and really make his day by telling him that by virtue of the gifting laws, I would like to cut a check in his name for $14,000 that would be totally income, gift and estate tax free.

Of course, doing so may not be the wisest move. But it would be very effective in shrinking one's estate. Consider how such a gift would benefit those you really care about, at the same time reducing your estate annually by the amount of the gift. A married couple can each gift this allowance, meaning that they could gift up to $28,000 per year per beneficiary. A couple with five children, five grandchildren and two great grand-grandchildren, can gift up to $336,000 per year. By maximizing this tax free strategy annually, one's estate could shrink with relative ease. That is, of course, if the growth doesn't outpace the gifts.

Annual gifts are a "use it or lose it" proposition, with no carry forward provisions. Another option to consider is transferring all or a portion of your lifetime gift allowance, currently unified with the estate tax exclusion of $5.25 million. By establishing an Integrated Dynasty Trust, you will be able to retain control, continue to receive income and <u>FREEZE</u> the transferred asset so that all future growth is out of your estate. Of course, once you have used your lifetime gift you cannot use it again when you die. Transferring your lifetime exclusion in an Integrated Dynasty Trust is an advanced estate planning strategy and should be discussed with a top notch estate planning attorney. Call us toll-free for a referral.

True, some might question the wisdom of gifting these funds to your family while they are young, believing that if they start to depend on the annual or lifetime gift they will become counterproductive. However, there is no law requiring that the recipients actually have to receive the gift in cash; nor do they need to have access to the gift immediately.

Solution:

By transferring the gift inside an irrevocable trust, such as a Spousal Support Family Dynasty Trust (SSFDT), an Integrated Family Dynasty Trust (IFDT), or an Irrevocable Life Insurance Trust (ILIT), it can be stipulated that while the gift is given today, it cannot be accessed until certain parameters are achieved, or the recipient reaches a given age. You should maintain as much control as you can over these gifts for as long as possible. Never let your beneficiaries dictate what should be done with your gift to them as this usually spells disaster. You are the benefactor and should always maintain control, even after you are gone.

Another idea: rather than giving the gift outright to your heirs today to do with it as they please, invest today's gift in something that immediately multiplies. This strategy is known as "The Gift Tax Leverage Coupon".

For example, if a couple, aged 65, set aside a simple gift of $28,000 a year to just one child, that money would mushroom to over $3,000,000 of tax-free cash for delivery when the surviving spouse dies (see Figure 2). This is accomplished by establishing a Joint and Survivor Life Insurance policy inside an ILIT, SSDT, or an IFDT and using the gift each year to pay the insurance premium. The proceeds could be used to pay future or income taxes, create a guaranteed estate, replace assets gifted to charities or cover debt. An enhanced version of The Gift Tax Leverage Coupon

(GTLC) is found in *The Family Bank Strategy* that is explained in detail in Mistake 8 on page 62.

This GTLC concept is easy, effective and can allow your estate to remain intact and out of the hands of the federal government. To see how the "Gift Tax Leverage Coupon" can work for you, give us a call, toll-free 1-888-892-1102, and we'll prepare your personalized illustration specific for your situation.

Mistake 6:

Not properly preparing for the exorbitant cost of long-term medical care

According to the Health Insurance Association of America, roughly 70% of Americans over age 65 will require some form of long-term care and 30% will require nursing home care. At a national average annual cost of $90,000 for a nursing home, $70,000 for home care and $43,000 for an assisted living facility, a lengthy illness could wipe out many estates, especially considering that before you can be eligible for government financial assistance for long-term care, you must first "spend down" your assets.

"Have you taken any steps to shield your investments from the vicious arm of the medical industry?"

Are you prepared to take the chance that your assets will endure the potential costs of long term illness or an accident? Have you taken any steps to shield your investments from the vicious arm of the medical industry?

My Great Aunt Mary took care of my brothers and me when my mother worked outside the home. She was a wonderful, loving caregiver. Later in life, she contracted severe arthritis and Alzheimer's, requiring constant care. My mother and her sister would take turns caring for Aunt Mary, rotating every year. She had a modest estate, but she was proud of what she had put away and made it known that the money was going to my mother and aunt for their benevolent guardianship. The money was to be her legacy and payback.

As her health declined, it became painfully obvious that we couldn't adequately care for her by ourselves. We needed help. Furthermore, my usually active parents were confined to the house in order to provide the vigilance that Aunt Mary's condition needed. After months of worrying, the difficult decision was reached; Aunt Mary would be admitted into a nearby

David T. Phillips

nursing home to receive the constant care she deserved. It was a tough choice, but ultimately the best for all concerned.

Then reality hit. Where was the money going to come from to pay for her stay? We were asked to complete a financial statement in which her savings and investments were listed. The nursing home informed us that before Medicaid would give a dime, Mary's small fortune – Mom's and Auntie's inheritance – would have to be used.

Yes, it was a blessing that she had the foresight to save some money for her "rainy day," but was it what she really wanted? Was her goal to have her assets confiscated in order to qualify for Medicaid's long-term medical care assistance? Even modest estates need planning.

Solution:

Four simple words – LONG-TERM CARE INSURANCE. If you are relatively healthy and between the ages of 50-80, you are an ideal candidate for long-term care insurance (LTCI). The premiums however are pricey, are considered an expense, a "use it or lose it" proposition, and underwriting approval can be a significant challenge.

Fortunately, there are a few insurance carriers that are now offering an avant-garde long-term care strategic power move referred to as the **Asset Based Care Plan or Hybrid LTC Combo plans.**

One of the plans I recommend, known as *The Life/LTC Strategy*, includes the following features:

- You can transfer a lump sum – CD/money market, or elect to make annual deposits;
- An immediate life insurance benefit that significantly increases your initial deposit (65 year old male: $100,000 = $225,000);
- Monthly long term medical care benefit is equal to 2% of the life insurance benefit, ($225,000 life insurance benefit = $4,500 per month benefit for 50 months). Any balance is paid out tax-free to your beneficiaries;
- Tax deferred cash accumulation;

- The tax-free monthly LTC benefit is an indemnity benefit (no receipts required) and can be sent to any country in the world.
- Tax-free income distribution if you select the contributory option;
- Minimum 2% guaranteed interest to hedge potential market losses;
- Three distinct investment choices, including the extremely popular Multi-Indexed Strategy to increase your cash account balance.

The Life/LTC Strategy offers a rare three-for-one: 1) Life Insurance, 2) Tax-free Accumulation and 3) Long Term Medical protection, making it virtually needless to spend your savings to purchase a standalone Long Term Care Policy.

Another plan I really like is the *Annuity/LTC Combo*. With this plan you take a liquid asset and transfer into a federally approved and HIPAA compliant single premium annuity where it will earn tax-deferred interest. Should you trigger the long term medical provision by not being able to perform 2 of the 6 activities of daily living (ADLs) or are cognitively impaired, your annuity value will explode up to three times and will create a TAX-FREE monthly long term benefit that will be paid out over 5 to 11 years.

Should you be fortunate and never trigger the LTC benefit, the annuity value will pass to your beneficiaries, unlike the "use it or lose it" stand alone LTC policies.

With both the Life/LTC Strategy and the Annuity/LTC Strategy you are taking an unproductive asset and exchanging it for a "safe-money" investment that will make certain you will not need to dip into your other assets to take care of a potential financially devastating long term illness or medical condition.

How to turn Tax-Deferred into Tax-Free: As of January 1, 2010, President Bush's *2006 Pension Protection Act* (PPA) stipulated that you can take withdrawals from an annuity Tax-Free, as long as the withdrawals are used for Long Term Care expenses. The caveat is your annuity must be PPA compliant and meet all of the Long Term Care Annuity requirements. As of 2013, there are only a few annuities that meet the PPA LTC/Annuity qualifications. Those that do, provide an excellent opportunity to turn old tax-deferred annuities into tax-free long term care income.

It's not uncommon for us to come across clients who have deferred taking withdrawals from their annuities for 10, 15 even 20 or more years. I've seen some with as high as 500% gain because most folks simply don't want to bite the annuity income tax bullet. Unfortunately all of that tax-deferred gain is taxed on a – Last In First Out (LIFO) basis – at your ordinary income tax rate. It's no wonder less than 10% of all annuity money is actually withdrawn during the annuitant's lifetime.

The power play is to do what is called a IRC Section 1035 tax-free exchange. Move your old annuity with built up gain into a PPA compliant LTC/Annuity. You'll not only leverage your deposit to increase its' value up to three times in Long Term Care Benefits, but you'll also be able to withdraw those benefits 100% tax-free.

CALL TO ACTION: Call today 1-888-899-1102 to request a personalized Hybrid LTC Combo Strategy Comparative Analysis.

Mistake 7:

Failure to properly plan the distribution of your pension/retirement accounts

How would you like to toil your entire life, build a sizeable estate with $1 million in your IRA that you had rolled over from the lump sum you received at retirement from General Electric, only to have Uncle Sam confiscate $700,000 of it at your death? **That's 70% gone forever!** Nobody wants that, and yet, an alarming 80% of all pension/IRA monies are transferred at death – and thus taxed – to named beneficiaries. That means only 20% of the nation's IRA monies are actually used as retirement income.

In other words, we build our fortune, set aside our pension money to provide a safety blanket for us just in case we need it, and then usually don't touch it. The problem is compounded by the fact that, because of investment gains, these retirement funds can grow to astronomical numbers. IRAs in excess of $3 million aren't rare these days. Yet only a few investment advisors, accountants and stockbrokers know the art of extracting these funds or passing them to the next generation without the government first tearing away the lion's share. That's because most are unaware of what I call the **Five Retirement Time Bombs**.

The first three time bombs explode during our lifetime.

1. Income tax. Up to 40% of federal income tax (plus state tax where applicable) is levied on distributions made during lifetime.
2. The "too early" 10% tax. Distributions of taxable qualified assets before age 59½ are subject to an additional 10% excise tax intended to discourage spending tax-subsidized retirement savings before retirement.
3. The "too late, too little" or 50% penalty tax. A 50% penalty is imposed for a failure to distribute a minimum amount of qualified assets each year beginning at the participants required beginning date (April 1) following the year in which they turn

70 ½. This is known as the **required minimum distribution (RMD).**

The last two bombs detonate after death.

4. Income in respect of a decedent (IRD).
Accounts are taxed for income in respect of a decedent (IRD) if distributed to the named beneficiaries after the death of the participant. Before 2007, only a spouse was allowed to roll over the inherited retirement account into their own personal IRA. But now *all* beneficiaries can do the same (stretch) as long as they follow certain, recently introduced IRS guidelines allowing them to spread their inherited IRA over their lifetime.

5. Estate tax/death tax. We've discussed this time bomb already. But as it relates to retirement funds, take note: The worst thing you can do is require that your heirs pay the estate taxes with your retirement account. Not only will they be paying the estate taxes – federal and state – they will also be required to pay income taxes on the funds used to pay the estate taxes. *This could result in an automatic*

loss of 70% of the overall value of your retirement account.

Solution:

<u>Spend it!</u> That should be the first order of business. When you turn 70½, the government requires that you begin extracting required minimum distributions based on the published RMD table. If you fail to take your RMD, as previously stated, a tax bomb of 50% is imposed.

I love the bumper sticker on those massive RVs that reads, "I'm driving my children's inheritance." That's the way it should be. But, if your investments do well, it can be very difficult to spend it fast enough.

"The worst thing you can do is require that your heirs pay the funds from taxes with your retirement accounts."

Think about this. A $3 million IRA growing at 5 percent will produce $150,000 in annual income. Some retirees find it difficult to spend that kind of money and, as such, their estate keeps growing and the

TAX TIME BOMBS keep on ticking. So what's the real solution?

First, unless you have a prenuptial agreement, your spouse should always be the first in line as your primary beneficiary so he or she can roll the funds into their own IRA at your death. *If you are married, never name a Revocable Living Trust as the beneficiary* or *"To My Estate."* In each situation, the surviving spouse may have to pay income tax in the year received.

Second, by virtue of recent tax law changes, distributions from a deceased taxpayer's IRA/401k can now be made in one of three options: 1) a single upfront lump sum, 2) spread over a five-year period, or *3) over the life expectancy of the non-spouse beneficiary after rolling the inherited funds into a separate new individual IRA.*

Prior to 2001, all IRA/401k beneficiaries were required to pay full income taxes at their tax bracket the year after receiving their inheritance or over five years. This included the surviving spouse. Now, the income tax liability can be spread or *stretched* over the

David T. Phillips

beneficiary's lifetime. Furthermore, because of the *stretch* concept, you can now predetermine how and when the money is to be received. In other words, you can now control it and its distribution for **multiple generations.** The only hitch; you need to plan today while you are here. When you are gone, it's too late.

Call to action: If you are currently not withdrawing more than your RMD from your IRA/401k; if you have multiple beneficiaries with different needs and personalities; if you want to control distributions to some or all of your beneficiaries; if someone other than your spouse could possibly inherit your retirement accounts – *call us today* toll-free at 1-888-892-1102 for a complimentary copy of a Special Report titled: IRA Required Minimum Distribution Leveraged Strategy, which explains in detail how you can significantly amplify your RMD to benefit your children, grandchildren and even your great grandchildren.

Because of the law changes created by the Pension Protection Act of 2006, it is vital that you not only have your estate analyzed, but you should also review the overall soundness of your retirement plan.

Furthermore, you should absolutely have a "Distribution Expert" review your qualified accounts (IRA, 401K, 403B) *beneficiary forms* to make certain your wishes will be carried out. Call 1-888-892-1102 today. Without proper planning, you may be needlessly giving the major share of your life's earnings to the government.

TAX ALERT: During the past few years Congress has been considering changing the rules of engagement with regard to the distribution of qualified funds (IRA, 403b, 401k), to non-spousal beneficiaries (children and grandchildren). Currently, any beneficiary can "Stretch" the distributions and therefore the taxes over their lifetime.

Considering the huge national debt and the fact that there is an estimated **$16 trillion in IRA** and retirement funds alone, Congress cannot continue to allow non-spousal beneficiaries the luxury of "Stretching" the distribution over their lifetime. The federal government needs the tax revenue now. Several bills have recently been presented to Congress on this issue; furthermore, it was included in President Obama's 2014 Budget Proposal. You can expect that

David T. Phillips

very soon Congress will pass a law to tax these accounts over a **maximum of 5 years**. You need to prepare for this inevitability by creating liquidity to pay the tax bill.

IRA Required Minimum Distribution Table

Age	IRS Distribution Factor	Age	IRS Distribution Factor
70	27.4	93	9.6
71	26.5	94	9.1
72	25.6	95	8.6
73	24.7	96	8.1
74	23.8	97	7.6
75	22.9	98	7.1
76	22.0	99	6.7
77	21.2	100	6.3
78	20.3	101	5.9
79	19.5	102	5.5
80	18.7	103	5.2
81	17.9	104	4.9
82	17.1	105	4.5
83	16.3	106	4.2
84	15.5	107	3.9
85	14.8	108	3.7
86	14.1	109	3.4
87	13.4	110	3.1
88	12.7	111	2.9
89	12.0	112	2.6
90	11.4	113	2.4
91	10.8	114	2.1
92	10.2	115 or older	1.9

Call today: 1.888.892.1102 to discuss how you can significantly multiply your annual RMD for your spouse, children and grandchildren through our proprietary RMD Leverage Strategy.

David T. Phillips

Mistake 8:

Lacking liquidity to cover estate settlement expenses

On the day you expire, there will be a financial assessment. Whether you have debt, owe taxes, need to replace your income, have legal fees or owe probate fees, your heirs will need cash. Consider these facts:

- 70% of today's affluent Americans don't have a sound estate plan;
- 52% do not have any life insurance at all;
- Of the 48% that do have insurance, they are only insured on average for 2.7 times their annual income, experts recommend a minimum 8 to 10 times;
- The majority of assets are not liquid;

- The economic downturns of 2001, 2002 and 2008 have exposed the vulnerability of non-guaranteed assets;
- Americans are living longer and are in serious danger of running out of money.

It is statistics like these that truly concern me. The lack of liquidity coupled with the insecurity of the markets, uncertainty of estate tax laws, unfounded bias and longevity have created the "perfect storm." Future generations of Americans will pay the price for our lack of motivation unless we wake up and become proactive.

Term life insurance is a vital estate planning tool when protecting the loss of your income while raising your family, covering debt or insuring any temporary need. But Term has its' limitations. At some point, when the term period expires, coverage either becomes cost prohibitive or unavailable.

The other day I was working with a family in Iowa on their estate plan. The parents were now in their 70's with a farm valued well over $15 million, with zero liquidity. The husband was now uninsurable due to an illness. They had acquired a term policy on his life to pay the future estate tax liability, but unfortunately that policy was set to expire in four years. Term Insurance is a viable option when used to insure temporary needs, but creating leveraged estate liquidity is not temporary.

After presenting to them the virtues of permanent insurance the wife lamented, "I wish we would have met you when we were healthy and younger. It is evident that we will outlive our term policies and be left with no protection."

Now with the federal estate tax exclusion at $5.25 million many will let their guard down and assume that their children and grandchildren will not have a tax liability. That may be so today, but remember it isn't the tax exclusion today that counts, it is the exclusion amount that is in effect when you pass away that matters. Furthermore, we need to account for investment growth. At 7%, an investment will double every 10 years. It is the wise person that plans for the worst and prays for the best.

Of equal concern is the income tax liabilities that will be created with qualified accounts (IRAs, 401k) when they are passed to non-spousal beneficiaries. In addition there is the matter of state inheritance tax (26 states currently impose a state transfer tax at death). Where is the cash going to come from to pay these taxes?

Which assets will be sold first? Faced with time constraints, (heirs have nine months to come in with the cash) will they command top dollar?

What if the markets decline during liquidation? Will the family summer cabin survive the tentacles of the IRS? These are the type of questions we will force our heirs to answer if we don't have a strategic plan in place beforehand.

If you are fortunate to have sufficient liquidity, such as cash or highly marketable securities, your heirs could theoretically use those assets to pay the bills, including taxes. But is that really prudent? Isn't there a better way than paying 100 cents on each dollar?

David T. Phillips

Solution:

A well planned life insurance portfolio should be in every estate. The only exception is the individual that is totally uninsurable, but that in and of itself is a mistake, because at some point in everyone's life they are insurable. Some just miss the boat because they didn't understand the leverage power of life insurance.

As stated previously, term insurance is a vital strategic tool that should be in estates with young children, debt and other temporary needs. But when the need for coverage ends, so should the policy.

For the past decade estate planners have used low cost Guaranteed Lifetime Permanent Insurance, with minimum premium and maximum coverage to create instant tax-free liquidity. We refer to this concept as *The Wealth Creation Strategy.* However, with the implementation of Regulation AG-38 on January 1, 2013 by the insurance commissioners of America, the products that we used for The Wealth Creation Strategy are not as attractive as they were prior to the premium increase. Furthermore, they are mostly one dimensional, designed primarily to create an instant and a guaranteed lifetime life insurance benefit.

I have always espoused the benefits of permanent insurance. But lately because of the closing of other available income tax loopholes permanent life insurance with its unique tax advantages has moved to the top of the leader board.

I consider it as a multi-dimensional "safe money" investment that should be inside every estate plan.

The Family Bank Strategy

Let me give you an example. A few months ago, Don a 72 year old patriarch of a family asked me to analyze his estate. His wife Janet was 67; both were in relatively good health. After everything was tabulated, it was determined that based on current values, their total estate was valued at a little over $3 million. Not a gigantic estate, but still in the top 1% of all Americans. I assured them that while there would be an income tax levied payable by their children, on their $800,000 IRA of as much as $300,000, if they didn't spend it first, there most likely wouldn't be a federal estate tax.

I then proceeded to introduce to them the multi-dimensional *Family Bank Strategy* that they immediately implemented. At 72, his $800,000 IRA required minimum distribution will be $31,250 this year. He wasn't using his RMD to live on, so he decided to leverage this money to fund his *Family Bank Strategy* over 10 years. The results were amazing:

- An **immediate** Supercharged Joint and Survivor life insurance benefit of $1,000,000. The $1,000,000 will pass to their children and grandchildren income and estate tax free through a special Irrevocable Dynasty Trust (IDT) that we arranged for them.
- A **future** Supercharged Joint and Survivor life insurance benefit of $1,000,000 that will be **paid up** in 10 years. That $1,000,000 will pass to their family income and estate tax free through their IDT. No matter what happens to their investments, interest rates or to the real estate market, no matter how much of their estate they spend. The Family Bank Strategy

will provide the cash their family can use to pay future taxes or simply guarantee an inheritance.

- A **tax-free cash accumulation** account that will become their personal *Family Bank*. In the future, should they need to access funds to supplement their retirement, they would be able to do so INCOME TAX-FREE. Furthermore, should family members need funds for emergencies education or opportunities, etc., the cash withdrawals will be available, via their trustee's authorization, totally INCOME TAX-FREE.

- A Tax-free wealth accumulation account that is tied to the "upside only" earnings of a stock market indexed.

Since the money to fund their Family Bank was coming from Don's RMD, it was as if he was converting the income to a Roth, but a Roth on Steroids. Let me explain: Had he taken the $31,250 RMD and simply invested it, all he would have to show for it would be the value of the investment account. By establishing the Family Bank Strategy he has created an instant $1,000,000 life insurance benefit

David T. Phillips

and a viable "safe money" investment that participates in the "upside only" of a stock market index.

Don and Janet's Family Bank Strategy
10 years: $399,128
15 years: $550,543
20 years: $744,163
*assuming an indexed return of 6.65%

Let's fast forward 10 years. Don and Janet's granddaughter Abby, who is now 11, celebrates her 21st birthday by announcing to the family that she has been accepted to medical school. After the congratulatory celebration she asks the big question, "How am I going to pay my tuition?" Don answers with assurance, "Let's take your annual tuition from the Family Bank, that's why we created it." By virtue of the policy loan provision they borrow the tuition from the insurance company each year, using the Family Bank's life insurance policy cash value as collateral, and receiving the funds **income tax-free** and **cost free**. You read it right… income tax free and cost free!

Don then tells Abby, "When you graduate and begin to make a decent living you can pay the money back into the Family Bank if you want." In reality if she doesn't pay the loan back, it would eventually be subtracted from the gross life insurance benefit, which would have been part of Abby's inheritance someday in the future.

The Family Bank Strategy can provide cash for schooling, a new business, a real estate opportunity, a down payment on a home, a quick start in life, etc. By using the unique provisions a properly designed permanent life insurance can afford, even your retirement income can be TAX-FREE. A true **Family Bank!**

Another client recently asked that I set up the Family Bank Strategy for them. To their disappointment it was determined that neither spouse was insurable. Since their goal really wasn't to provide the guaranteed life insurance benefit for their children because they were well off, it was decided that we would create a guaranteed inheritance and Family Bank Strategy for their grandchildren. We insured the two healthiest children for over $1,000,000 each by transferring his RMD and creating a tax-free Family Bank that can be used in the future for family emergencies or opportunities. Should either child pass away, the grandchildren's Irrevocable Dynasty Trust would receive a cash infusion of $1,000,000, income tax and estate tax free.

Important Notice: There can actually be a **fourth dimension** to The Family Bank Strategy. By insuring individuals instead of a couple with a Joint and Survivor policy, you can add a Long Term Medical Benefit rider that will generate a tax-free long term care benefit up to $10,000 per month that is derived from the life insurance benefit that was mentioned in Mistake 6.

Should you ever be in a position where you cannot perform 2 of the 6 Activities of Daily Living or you become cognitively impaired you can access the life insurance benefit for a period of 50 months, tax-free. Should you dodge the LTC bullet throughout your life, which is everyone's goal, your beneficiaries would eventually receive the life insurance proceeds, creating a win – win opportunity for you and your family.

Neither The Family Bank Strategy nor The Wealth Creation Strategy should be looked at as an expense. Both strategies should be viewed as simply the transferring of a portion of your assets into a different investment. This leveraged investment will produce a return that pales any other "safe money" investment.

Call to action: To understand this concept more fully, call *Estate Planning Specialists* toll-free at 1-888-892-1102 and request your complimentary personalized illustration.

The Family Bank Strategy
Joint & Survivor Version

Insured's Age - Health	$1,000,000 Tax-Free Life Insurance Benefit			
	Continuous Deposit		10 - Deposit	
55/55	$6,057		$11,462	
Male – Pfd	10th Yr. CV	20th Yr. Cv	10th Yr. CV	20th Yr. Cv
Female - Pfd	$56,458	$191,189	$133,166	$257,706
65/65	$11,099		$19,820	
Male – Pfd	10th Yr. CV	20th Yr. Cv	10th Yr. CV	20th Yr. Cv
Female - Pfd	$117,039	$347,957	$241,204	$442,055
75/75	$20,943		$33,904	
Male – Pfd	10th Yr. CV	20th Yr. Cv	10th Yr. CV	20th Yr. Cv
Female - Pfd	$224,127	$550,764	$410,578	$665,269

*Assuming index crediting rate of 6.65%

David T. Phillips

The Wealth Creation Strategy/Family Bank Strategy Individual Life Versions

Insured's Age - Health	$1,000,000 Tax-Free Life Insurance Benefit Continuous Deposit			
Age 55 – Preferred N/T	Male		Female	
	$12,905		$11,419	
	10th Yr. CV	20th Yr. Cv	10th Yr. CV	20th Yr. Cv
	$79,369	$208,286	$72,996	$183,834
Age 65 – Preferred N/T	Male		Female	
	$25,343		$20,360	
	10th Yr. CV	20th Yr. Cv	10th Yr. CV	20th Yr. Cv
	$157,237	$359,261	$137,950	$342,844
Age 75 – Preferred N/T	Male		Female	
	$51,409		$41,483	
	10th Yr. CV	20th Yr. Cv	10th Yr. CV	20th Yr. Cv
	$302,253	$532,043	$276,074	$529,806

*Assuming index crediting rate of 6.65%

Insured's Age - Health	$1,000,000 Tax-Free Life Insurance Benefit 10 - Deposit			
Age 55 – Preferred N/T	Male		Female	
	$23,802		$21,359	
	10th Yr. CV	20th Yr. Cv	10th Yr. CV	20th Yr. Cv
	$96,973	$330,535	$203,181	$297,368
Age 65 – Preferred N/T	Male		Female	
	$41,604		$34,869	
	10th Yr. CV	20th Yr. Cv	10th Yr. CV	20th Yr. Cv
	$382,245	$528,235	$333,095	$489,703
Age 75 – Preferred N/T	Male		Female	
	$68,647		$59,378	
	10th Yr. CV	20th Yr. Cv	10th Yr. CV	20th Yr. Cv
	$600,074	$728,663	$547,455	$703,348

*Assuming index crediting rate of 6.65%

Mistake 9:

Estate Shrinkage due to investments losses

If one of your goals is to actually leave your heirs an inheritance, you should consider the overall safety of your investment portfolio. Too often we see sizeable estates reduced to ashes overnight because of risky investments.

Back on March 10, 2000 the NASDAQ composite reached its all time high of **5,132**. By October 10, 2002 it had fallen to just **1,108**. A hypothetical **$100,000** invested during its high and held to its low, would have fallen to a dismal **$21,590**. That's a loss of more than **78%**! To make matters worse, it would require a return of **463%** growth just to break even. Assuming

8% return, it would take nearly **20 years** to recoup the loss.

Financial advisors generally recommend that the older we are the more we should have in safe investments. For every year of age an equal corresponding percentage should be in non-risk investments. For example a 70 year old's investment mix should be 70% in safe guaranteed investments and 30% at risk.

Today, finding that 70% "safe money" is becoming harder and harder to uncover. With market interest rates near all-time lows, is it really considered "safe" to take the traditional route and invest in bonds? Remember the value of your bonds decrease as interest rates rise. With the 10-Year Treasury Note at less than 2%, there is only one direction rates can go...up. Conversely, one direction for your bonds.

So where can you invest today that offers true safety on the downside should we experience severe market corrections, yet offers enough upside growth potential to combat the eroding purchasing power caused from inflation? I'll give you a hint: You won't find it at your local bank. CDs paying 1% and money markets paying 0.05% aren't going to help.

Solution:

Fortunately, today the financial industry has created new investment opportunities installed with safety guardrails that allow you to participate in market linked returns without the risk of plummeting into peril.

These "safe money" vehicles are Indexed Annuity and Indexed Universal Life. With both products you'll earn income tax-deferred stock market-linked interest returns if the market goes up. But if the market goes down, you are guaranteed to never lose a dime. This guarantee is made possible because of four specific guardrail features:

- First, your principal is backed by the assets of the insurance company issuing your Indexed Annuity or Indexed Universal Life.
- Second, you are contractually guaranteed to earn a minimum amount of interest each year – No Matter What!

David T. Phillips

- Third, all upside growth is locked in periodically (you select the time frame, usually on an annual basis) with no possibility of ever losing any gains you earn.
- Fourth, recent improvements have been made to both strategies, offering the option to generate a lifetime income stream for both you and your spouse. These new provisions can be set to guarantee a growth rate as high as 7% on the balance that derives your future income payments. Even if you live to the age of Methuselah, your pension like guaranteed income will continue to pay, month after month as long as you live!

Indexed Annuities and Indexed Universal Life are the only products that provide both a guarantee on the downside and upside potential. It is for this reason Mark Skousen, editor of *Forecast and Strategies* recently stated, "In my opinion, now would be a great time to take some of your chips off the table and lock-in your gains with an Indexed Annuity or Indexed Universal Life."

Call 1-888-892-1102 and ask our "safe money" specialists for our Special Report: *The Future of Retirement Savings* and for insights on today's top Indexed Annuities and Indexed Universal Life plans.

David T. Phillips

Mistake 10:

The improper use of jointly held property

For some reason, many feel that if they transfer ownership of their holdings to a close relative, the transaction will side step probate. Perhaps they saw this strategy on some movie or heard about it on a talk show. Don't be tempted! If your joint tenant or co-owner is sued or files bankruptcy, creditors will attack your valued asset and you will lose it, even if it is your home. Furthermore, a spouse from a second marriage could totally disinherit children from a previous marriage. Again, proper prior planning avoids these mishaps, but it does require thought and action.

Solution:

A professionally drafted Revocable Living Trust (estates under $500,000), Revocable Family Dynasty Trust (estates in excess of $500,000) avoid probate, after assets have been transferred into the trust, and gives you control after you depart this world. Your wishes will not only be carried forth, they cannot be contested if the trust is properly drafted.

A will, no matter how intricately designed, is always subject to probate and the associated costs. In addition, a will can be contested and becomes public knowledge. Drafted correctly, a RLT and a RFDT can be totally insulated.

The Durfee Law Group, a national firm has designed an extremely economical, easy-to-implement system that provides the basic tools virtually every estate should have in place. Tools such as a Revocable Family Dynasty Trust, Credit Shelter Trust, QTIP Trust, Pour-Over Will, Medical Power of Attorney, Durable Power of Attorney, IRA Dynasty Trust, Irrevocable Life Insurance Trust, Spousal Support Irrevocable Trust, Multi-Generational Trust, Integrated

David T. Phillips

Dynasty Trust etc. To receive further information and/or to receive their Client Profile Form, simply contact them at 1-480-324-8000 or by email to rick@durfeelawgroup.com. Mention this book to receive the Estate Planning Specialist Discount. Estate planning really can be that easy.

Conclusion:

Procrastination will be dangerous to your wealth

Why is it that the vast majority (70%) of America's affluent fail to successfully distribute their assets to the next generation? Why haven't you properly planned your estate?

There isn't just one answer. Fear, lack of education, cost, denial, etc., all contribute to one human trait — **procrastination**.

Webster defines **procrastination** as: "postponing or deferring taking action." I must admit I have fallen victim to procrastination just like any other human being. I even have daily, weekly, monthly and annual checklists and often time the item in question has been

David T. Phillips

on my list for ages. It happens to all of us. *But when you procrastinate your estate planning... eventually there isn't a tomorrow to turn to.*

Estate Planning Specialist, LLC was established in 1988 to make **ESTATE PLANNING EASY!** Visit our website: www.epmez.com to review comments from experts and a few of our clients. They, along with thousands of other clients, all started their estate plan at the beginning by sending in our *easy-to-complete* one page **Estate Analysis Profile** which provides us the information necessary to produce your professional, personalized **Estate Analysis.**

To get started and obtain your Estate Analysis Profile form simply log on to www.epmez.com, or call our toll free number **1-888-892-1102,** or complete the *Estate Planning Solutions Suite* Request Form on the next page and fax it to 1-480-899-6723. It's that easy.

Your Estate Planning Checklist:

25 Things you can do to get your estate in order.

One of the greatest gifts you can leave your posterity is an organized estate. The time you spend now will help your loved ones to cope later and ensure your wishes will be carried out. Here is a simplified checklist to help you get started on organizing your estate. It's a good idea to discuss your plans with your loved ones and the executor of your will. You'll also want to consult with your legal and tax advisers. If you currently do not have a legal advisor, contact The Durfee Law Group at 1.480.324.8000 for a complimentary initial consultation.

David T. Phillips

Estate Planning

1. ☐ Make or update your will. A will allows you to determine what happens to your money and possessions when you die, and who becomes the guardian of your minor children. A will should be included in every estate plan, no matter the size, otherwise, state laws and courts make those decisions for you.

2. ☐ Make a living will. This document can speak for you by outlining the medical procedures you want taken if you become too ill to state your wishes yourself.

3. ☐ Create durable powers of attorney. These documents allow you to appoint someone to make decisions on your behalf if you become incapacitated. There are two types: one to deal with your personal, legal and financial affairs, and another to deal with health-care decisions.

4. ☐ Create a letter of instruction. This document provides a list of instructions for your survivors to follow. For example, it can spell out funeral wishes, people to contact, and where your will, trust and other key papers can be

found. It also can provide information about your financial accounts and activities.

5. ☐ **Calculate your net worth, including life insurance proceeds.** If you have substantial net worth, call us toll free 1-888-892-1102 to discuss the necessary steps to minimize or eliminate the impact of federal and state estate taxes and income taxes.

6. ☐ **Establish a Revocable Family Dynasty Trust (RFDT) if appropriate.** A RFDT is a legal entity that holds property designated by you for the benefit of you and your beneficiaries. A RFDT also avoids the expense and publicity of probate. You should seriously consider establishing a RFDT if your estate is greater than $500,000. If your estate is valued less than $500,000 a simple Revocable Living Trust will suffice. Furthermore, if you have minor children as your primary heirs or if they are named as your life insurance beneficiaries (legally they are too young to receive proceeds directly) - you should have a Revocable Family Dynasty Trust.

7. ☐ **Consider funeral preplanning.** Preplanning

can relieve stress on your survivors and give you control over the ultimate cost of your funeral. If you are a U.S. military veteran, you may want military honors at your service; contact your local funeral home or military installation to check on eligibility and availability.

8. ☐ Make arrangements for the orderly transfer of business assets. Business owners can predetermine what will happen to assets through legal agreements and life insurance on business partners.

Insurance Planning

9. ☐ Buy or update your life insurance. Life insurance provides an immediate source of cash that is exempt from federal and state income tax (but, in general, not estate taxes). It is important to review your ownership, beneficiary and coverage amount every two or three years to make sure your policies still reflect your needs and wishes. You may want to consider establishing an Irrevocable Life Insurance Trust, Irrevocable Spouse Support Trust, or an Integrated Family Dynasty Trust to make

certain that all life insurance proceeds are not included in the total sum of your estate. Life insurance benefits are received income tax free, but are not estate tax free if you have any incidents of ownership.

10. ☐ Consider buying health/medical insurance. There are three major types of coverage that help protect and stretch your assets: Major Medical protects you against the ever-rising cost of medical care; and Disability Insurance that helps protect your income should you no longer be able to work. Long-Term Care Insurance that covers the cost of long term health care in your home or at a long-term care facility. You will want to review the new Hybrid LTC Combo Strategies as an alternative to traditional Long Term Care Insurance. As explained is Mistake 6.

11. ☐ Review your pension plan's survivor benefits. This might be a plan offered through your employer or the military's Survivor Benefit Plan (SBP).

12. ☐ Review your IRA, 401(k) and other retirement plans to make certain the correct beneficiary designation is in line with your wishes.

David T. Phillips

Organizing Financial Records

NOTE: If you store any of the following information on your computer, make a list of all passwords; indicate where any diskettes are stored and where the information can be found.

13. ☐ Create a list of financial accounts. List account numbers and pertinent information about your investments, bank accounts, insurance policies (life, disability, homeowners, credit and life) and other financial matters.

14. ☐ List the location of valuable documents. Your list might include deeds, car titles, military records, birth and marriage certificates, divorce decrees and estate planning documents.

15. ☐ List your personal data. This can include your Social Security number, driver's license number, VA claim number, your date of birth and the names and phone numbers of family members.

16. ☐ Make arrangements for access to your safe-deposit box. In many states, safe-deposit boxes are closed upon death and are not opened until probate. Make sure copies of your will and other important documents are available outside

of your safe-deposit box and allow co-access with one of your children or a trusted friend.

17. ☐ List loan payments. This listing should include information about credit cards, mortgages, consumer loans, and auto and personal loans.

18. ☐ List other income sources and government benefits. This includes pensions and Social Security. For information on military benefits, check with the Veteran's Administration.

19. ☐ List the location of tax records.

20. ☐ Verify account ownership and beneficiary designations. Check financial accounts and insurance policies to make sure these conform to your current estate planning objectives.

21. ☐ List all organizations in which you have membership. They may provide special death benefits and should be noted for your survivors.

Personal Planning

22. ☐ Provide a trusted family member or friend with the location of confidential or valuable items you may have put away for safekeeping.

23. ☐ Provide a family member or friend with the location of spare keys and security codes.

David T. Phillips

24. ☐ Provide easy access to your will, trusts and your durable powers of attorney. Keep signed, original copies in your attorney's office as well as a copy in a fireproof file at home. Also give a signed copy to your executor.

25. ☐ Provide the name of your veterinarian and care instructions for pets, if appropriate.

Estate Planning Test

If you answer yes to any of these questions, call us today: 1.888.892.1102 to begin your estate planning.

Y N

☐ ☐ Do you have children under 18 years of age?

☐ ☐ Are there marital complications from a previous marriage?

☐ ☐ Is a goal in your estate to pass on money/assets to your children?

☐ ☐ Is a goal in your estate to be taxed as little as legally possible?

☐ ☐ Would you like to limit the court systems involvement in your estate?

☐ ☐ Is your financial privacy a concern?

☐ ☐ Is anyone in your family disabled?

☐ ☐ Is there anyone in your family who is a citizen

David T. Phillips

in another country?

☐ ☐ Would you consider distributing your assets differently among your children?

☐ ☐ Do you have concerns with the spending habits of many of your children?

☐ ☐ Would there be disagreement among family members if everything was divided equally?

☐ ☐ Have you had your 5 Critical Estate Documents created?

☐ ☐ Is your estate going to be above the State and Federal exclusions?

☐ ☐ Do you know how to properly title your assets for tax benefit?

How to get started today:

Professionally plan your estate. With Estate Planning Solutions Suite you'll receive:

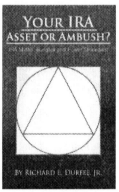

$19.95

Special Report: YOUR IRA Asset or Ambush - IRA Myths Bungles and Power Strategies: This 60 page Special Report will teach you how to "STRETCH" your IRA over multiple generations, protecting it from creditors, prior spouses, and life's crisis events. You'll discover how to take advantage of the new Required Minimum Distributions rules and how to minimize your tax liability. You will further learn how to integrate your IRA with your estate and financial

David T. Phillips

planning objectives and pass it to your family in the most tax efficient way possible.

Complimentary Legal Audit of Estate Planning Documents: A legal review by The Durfee Law Group of your estate planning **$300.00** documents, along with a follow-up conference. The following questions, as well as any others you may have will be answered in the review:

- Do your existing documents need updating?
- Is your plan accomplishing your current objectives?
- Does your existing plan account for changes in family or financial circumstances?
- Does your current plan minimize estate taxes?
- Is the wealth you pass to your spouse and children protected against their future creditors, divorces, or other crisis events?
- Does your plan have a protector?
- Does your plan pass your values on with your wealth?
- Does your plan incorporate a way to avoid and resolve disputes outside the courtroom?

$30.00

Estate Made Easy Book: Completely revised and updated, best selling *Estate Planning Made Easy* features all you need to know about current tax legislation to protect your family! Author David T. Phillips provides a compact but comprehensive guide to help you easily negotiate through the Estate Planning maze of confusion

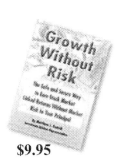

$9.95

Special Report: *Growth Without Risk*: This 40 page Special Report will show you how thousands are crash proofing their portfolios and earning stock market linked returns while locking in gains without market risk.

Special Report: Disinherit the IRS - This 20 page report was written to provide expert, objective advice on how to properly safeguard your assets from the IRS and preserve your posterity's financial independence. Among other strategies, it reveals how

$9.95

David T. Phillips

you can use the tremendous leverage and tax advantages of a powerful estate planning tool that will provide the necessary cash to avoid the federal confiscation of your assets and create guaranteed wealth, valued many times greater than your deposit transfer.

$397.00

Estate Planning Analysis – Your Estate Plan Road Map: This *personalized* comprehensive analysis will break down your current estate plan and provide recommendations that outline viable strategies specifically applicable to you. Included are calculations which graphically illustrate potential taxation, both current and projected, with side-by-side comparisons of proposed tax saving strategies.

Normally over **$774.00** when purchased separately, this comprehensive package, including the *Estate Planning Made Easy* book, Special Reports, your Personalized Estate Analysis, plus a Complimentary Legal Audit of your estate planning documents, is available for a limited time for only **$397** plus shipping & handling.

Order Your Estate Planning Solution Suite Today.

☐ **YES**, I want to take charge of my future today and protect my estate from excessive taxation and needless costs or hassle. Rush my Estate Planning Solutions Suite for just **$397** plus $9.95 for shipping.

Name	
Address	
City, State, Zip	
Day Phone	Evening Phone
Email Address	

With regard to estate planning, the *waiting game is the loser's game.* Don't put this off any longer, take charge of your estate planning now and call us toll-free at **1-888-892-1102,** or visit us on the web at

www.epmez.com.

Return this Request Form to:

Phillips Financial Services

2200 E. Williams Field Rd. Suite 200

Gilbert, AZ 85295

Fax to: 1-480-899-6723

David T. Phillips